OCTOBER
BY IAN WILDING

CURRENCY PRESS
The performing arts publisher
www.currency.com.au

CURRENCY PLAYS

First published in 2007
by Currency Press Pty Ltd,
PO Box 2287, Strawberry Hills, NSW, 2012, Australia
enquiries@currency.com.au
www.currency.com.au
in association with
Griffin Theatre Company, Sydney

Reprinted 2014, 2015, 2016

NATIONAL LIBRARY OF AUSTRALIA CIP DATA
    Wilding, Ian
       October.
       ISBN 9780868198026.
       I. Title.
    A822.4

Typeset by Dean Nottle for Currency Press.
Cover photograph by Mark Rogers.
Cover design by Jeremy Saunders.
Front cover shows Simone McAullay as Angela in the Griffin Theatre
Company production.

Currency Press acknowledges the Traditional Owners of the Country on which
we live and work. We pay our respects to all Aboriginal and Torres Strait
Islander Elders, past and present.

Contents

October was premiered by Griffin Theatre Company at the SBW Stables Theatre, Sydney, on 26 April 2007 with the following cast:

DICK	Simon Burke
ANGELA	Simone McAullay
TIM	Christopher Stollery
DEZ	Ed Wightman

Director, Julian Meyrick
Designer, Jo Briscoe
Lighting Designer, Bernie Tan
Sound Designer, Nick Wishart

October was developed as part of the Melbourne Theatre Company's Hard Lines Affiliate Writers' Scheme.

CHARACTERS

TIM, late 50s
ANGELA, 30s
DEZ
DICK

SCENE ONE

DEZ *and* ANGELA.

DEZ: I saw you. Yes. And you saw me. I said hello. And then you just walked past.

ANGELA: I'm sorry. I don't understand.

DEZ: You stopped. Looked the other way. And then walked past. You saw me then looked away. When I said hello. And I said it quite loud.

ANGELA: If you were shouting in the street I probably did look away. [*She laughs.*] If someone from nowhere comes up and shouts at you in the street—

DEZ: You looked me in the eye and then walked past. Like I was no one. And I want to know why. Because I am someone.

ANGELA: Are you? And is that something entirely up to you?

TIM *enters with a glass of water for* ANGELA.

TIM: And you're sure you won't have anything?

DEZ: Dez.

TIM *pours himself a tumbler of scotch.*

ANGELA: May I ask a stupid question?

DEZ: Go ahead.

TIM: [*with* DEZ] Go ahead—darling.

ANGELA: Only I haven't been introduced.

DEZ: We haven't been introduced.

ANGELA: I don't mean to be formal.

TIM: Is everything all right, darling?

ANGELA: I'm not entirely sure.

ANGELA *laughs.*

DEZ: We haven't been introduced. That's great.

TIM: That's great. What's great?

ANGELA: I don't mean to be rude. But I'm afraid we must be at cross purposes.

DEZ: That's fine. No I get it.

TIM: I'm confused.

ANGELA: Dez? Yes. Hello. Yes. I'm sorry. How to ask this? Am I supposed to know you?

DEZ: That's great.

ANGELA: It's just—where is it I'm supposed to know you from?

TIM: Yes. I'm confused.

DEZ: You would be.

ANGELA: But where is it you think you know me from?

DEZ: Do you want me to say it in front of your husband?

TIM: In front of me?

ANGELA: No. I'm sorry. I don't mean to be—

DEZ: Rude.

TIM: You told me you were a friend. Is that not the truth?

ANGELA: A friend of mine?

DEZ: I didn't say I was a friend.

TIM: I hope we're not going to split hairs. Because you take someone on their word—

DEZ: Jesus.

ANGELA: You seem upset. Is there something we can do to help you?

DEZ: There is, actually.

TIM: You don't know him?

ANGELA: No.

TIM: I take people at face value. And I let you in on your word. Now if there's been a mistake—fine. That happens.

ANGELA: I don't want you to feel that I'm saying anything by it—but I've never met you.

TIM: Are you selling something?

DEZ: If I was selling something I wouldn't come where the residents already have everything. Unless it was insurance.

TIM: Insurance?

DEZ: I'm not selling anything.

ANGELA: Are you from a religious group?

DEZ: Am I a fundamentalist?

ANGELA: We don't discriminate.

DEZ: I take communion. Is there a problem with that?

TIM: No. I don't understand.

DEZ: The sacrament.

ANGELA: We're saying we don't make judgements based on religion, Dez.

TIM: This is the wrong way to go about things.

ANGELA: It is a little unfair.

TIM: And you will achieve nothing by it.

ANGELA: Can we call someone for you? Is there someone who helps you?

TIM: You've made a cock-up. Yes? Don't worry about it.

ANGELA: Happens to the best of us.

TIM: You've made a stuff-up. Let's not make this embarrassing.

DEZ: I'm only human. I guess I'd like to hear you admit that much.

ANGELA: I do understand that.

DEZ: But you clearly don't.

ANGELA: Do you need some money?

DEZ: I haven't asked you for money.

ANGELA: I offered.

DEZ: I'm only human. That's what I asked for.

TIM: Look. Angela says she doesn't know you. And I certainly don't know you.

DEZ: Why certainly? Because I don't move in your circle? Because I didn't go to your school?

ANGELA: No.

TIM: Because we just don't.

DEZ: It's that simple.

TIM: There's been some sort of a mistake. It's that simple.

ANGELA: Or tell us how we can help you.

TIM: I have about two hundred dollars.

ANGELA: Just to help you out. We're offering. You didn't ask.

TIM: We are being civil about this. Yes?

DEZ: Women are a puzzle with no solution.

TIM: Look. Just sling your hook, mate.

DEZ: Sling my hook?

TIM: Not sling—

DEZ: Is that you or Johnny Walker talking?

TIM: No. This is Laphroaig.

ANGELA: A very good friend of ours is a life counsellor.

DEZ: That must make you very happy.

ANGELA: She specialises in cognitive behavioural therapy.

DEZ: And you are telling me because—

ANGELA: If you are feeling lost—confused. Is that the right word? The city is a big lonely thing.

TIM: It is.

DEZ: And ever more so.

ANGELA: And I'm sure she would talk to you—as a favour—if I asked her. And she works on a sliding scale.

DEZ: That's really fucking kind of you, Angela. No really. Really fucking generous.

ANGELA *exits.*

TIM: Listen to my exact words. Listen to my intonation. Don't become agitated. I am willing to drive you wherever it is you need to go. There are people who can help you. We are offering to put you in touch with the people or agencies who can help you with whatever it is that has you so—I will even drive you to your church. If you need to pray. But I would really like it—prefer it—if you were to just go. And now.

DEZ: I fucked her. I know. I fucked your wife. And we had more than that. Lovers? Is that going too far? I don't know. I don't think so. We sat on the edge of the bed and talked and laughed. I didn't know she was married. But the truth remains I fucked her.

TIM: Let me call you a cab. I'll pay for it.

DEZ: Don't you want to know what she's really like?

TIM: Not really. No.

DEZ: Right.

TIM: Listen carefully to what I am saying. Get help before this escalates.

DEZ: I will.

TIM: I broke a man's nose once. Yes I did. And it didn't give me any pleasure. But I would do it again.

DEZ: Going to get the old boy's rugby fifteen together and stand on my head until I agree with your version of the world?

TIM: You are in my home under false pretences. I have given you the benefit of the doubt. I took you in on your word. I won't creep through life. And so now I want you to go. Can you go now? You will go. And it will be now. Go. Now. I'm waiting.

ANGELA *enters.*

Angela. Call the police.

ANGELA: I have. I just did. [*To* DEZ] You need to be somewhere safe.

TIM: There is still time for us to organise transport to a clinic rather than a cell.

ANGELA: I only called the police because they will help you get wherever you need to be. Not to punish you. There's nothing to punish. Really.

DEZ: Once upon a time the future was full of possibility. But the future just ended. The future just died. And I didn't get a say in it. Then I saw you—quite by chance. And I said hello. We both knew. We stood there. Then you looked away. And then you walked.

TIM: Don't threaten us please. Don't threaten anyone.

ANGELA: We can see that you're hurting.

DEZ: I've seen things that I know are true. And so have you. You know the difference. [*To* ANGELA] Me and you. I'll see you again. And next time—you will see me. I'll make certain of it. I'll stand somewhere you can't look away and—pretend. I just wanted to know why. Yeah. I reckon I know. Enjoy all your stuff. While it lasts. And dance, you selfish fuckers, dance. [*Pause.*] Come with me. Come with me.

DEZ *exits.*

ANGELA: He doesn't know me—us. He doesn't know us. How can he—?

TIM *exits then re-enters.*

He doesn't know us. I didn't—I don't look away. How can he say those things when he doesn't even know us?

They embrace.

Did you lock the door?

♦ ♦ ♦ ♦ ♦

SCENE TWO

TIM *and* ANGELA.

TIM: I have to go in early tomorrow. To justify my fuel consumption.

ANGELA: You care too much.

TIM: People hate turbulence. I care about people. Shoot me for flying around it.

ANGELA: You're a fantastic pilot.

TIM: It's what I love.

ANGELA: It shows. And it shows that you care about people.

TIM: Which is why I fly around turbulence when I could just—

ANGELA: I know you do.

TIM: —save fuel by flying through it.

ANGELA: And as a shareholder I would prefer it if you did. [*She laughs.*] No.

TIM: The business demands. And the demands of people. It becomes harder to negotiate the opposites.

ANGELA: We had a whole new season of samples descend on us today.

TIM: You love it when a new season descends.

ANGELA: I think people should live in beautiful houses. Is that wrong?

TIM: No. They're lucky to have you.

ANGELA: Are they?

TIM: All the people you design for. [*He sips his drink then drops some ice into it.*] No. No.

ANGELA: No?

TIM: No. This is hopeless. This not saying is—

ANGELA: Yes. I know.

TIM: I can't pretend that nothing happened.

ANGELA: I love you.

TIM: It's just so—feeling like you can't say because certain words are off limits.

ANGELA: Did you hear me?

TIM: And I love you. And you know that.

ANGELA: I do.

TIM: But this random act of violence—

ANGELA: You know I would do anything for you, don't you?

TIM: And me for you.

ANGELA: There is nothing—no line.

TIM: And I feel exactly the same way.

> TIM *and* ANGELA *are together.*

ANGELA: You're shaking.

TIM: I am so angry, Angela.

ANGELA: Please. Don't be.

TIM: I don't want to be.

ANGELA: There's no point.

TIM: But I have to do something. A response of some sort.

ANGELA: Yes.

TIM: Because until we know what he is capable of—

ANGELA: I didn't want to call the police.

TIM: You had no choice.

ANGELA: They have a description at least. He could be an escaped anything.

TIM: That's true.

ANGELA: For his own good. He could hurt himself.

TIM: He'll cry foul. Victim of society. The product of an unjust system. Sad thing is it looks like it's true.

> ANGELA *stands with the phone.* TIM *has a sip from his tumbler of scotch.*

ANGELA: Shall I call James?

TIM: So he can write a stiff letter on the law-firm letterhead?

ANGELA: Just to get our legal position clear.

TIM: You won't get any sense out of him at this time. He'll be more than half cut.

ANGELA: The policeman is dropping in some leaflets tomorrow.

TIM: Leaflets?

ANGELA: On home security.

TIM: You take people on face value. You don't want to creep through life assuming—give people the benefit of the doubt. But this is violence. And random. And pointless.

ANGELA: It's horrible. But if he's ill—disenfranchised.

TIM: I mean what would you have to do with him?

ANGELA: I know. No. No I don't know what you mean.

TIM: Isn't that what he was saying?

ANGELA: He was saying—I don't know what he was saying.

TIM: You're a successful professional woman. An extraordinary interior designer.

ANGELA: Thank you.

TIM: What would you want with a man like that? I mean—what kind of man was he?

ANGELA: I don't know what he was thinking. I don't think he knows. Which is what is so sad.

TIM: Sad is the word.

ANGELA: I mean I am hurt. I could be simplistic and lash out.

TIM: But what would a woman like you want with a man like that?

ANGELA: I don't want anything with him.

TIM: Speaking hypothetically. What would there be? I'd really like to know.

ANGELA: I really don't want to think about it.

TIM: But seriously imagine it.

ANGELA: How could I know? Nothing.

TIM: He obviously thinks there is something.

ANGELA: Don't. Please.

TIM: Isn't that what he was driving at? That he knew you.

ANGELA: No. Don't.

TIM: Some dirty hotel room.

ANGELA: I don't go to dirty hotel rooms.

TIM: Yes.

ANGELA: I don't go to dirty hotel rooms. You of all people should know that.

TIM: Someone turns up at your door—with vile ideas. It's envy. It's jealousy. I don't know. But his hate is general. So he shouldn't be specific with his actions and single someone—us—out. So what do we do? Get the locks changed. Roller shutters. Alarms. Video camera. Panic room. Big dog. Up the security.

ANGELA: I simply said we should look at the pamphlets.

TIM: A fist. What is the correct word? If they want to follow you home— is there anything you can do? If they know where you live—does having more leaflets help—long term?

ANGELA: It was just a suggestion.

TIM: There is a whole world full of invisible people—

ANGELA: But it doesn't make it any easier not to be livid when they show up and single you out.

TIM: Yes. Thank you. Thank you for saying that.

> *He sips his drink.*

ANGELA: What am I going to do tomorrow?

TIM: We'll get the place fortified. We'll get a moat.

ANGELA: I have to go to people's houses on nothing more than a phone conversation.

TIM: And I don't know, Angela. I really don't know.

He sips his drink.

ANGELA: You think I'm overreacting.

TIM: Take some time off.

ANGELA: I don't want to take time off.

TIM: And you shouldn't have to. You mustn't.

ANGELA: It was your idea.

TIM: I'm just giving you breathing space.

ANGELA: I don't want to take time off.

TIM: You do realise if we'd hurt him it would be us who are criminals. That's what James will say. I'll speak to James— [*He tops up his drink.*] You're beautiful. You are so beautiful. [*He tops up his ice.*] Do you think we have post-traumatic stress? I better not have. They'd suspend me.

He sips his drink.

ANGELA: We should go to bed.

TIM: What's intolerable for me is the image he has put in my head.

ANGELA: Yes. We should go to bed.

TIM: I feel like an absolute fool for letting him in.

ANGELA: I know it's early. But would you mind if we went to bed?

TIM: I don't believe for one second what he said. I don't. I don't believe a goddamn filthy fucking word he said.

ANGELA: That makes me very happy.

TIM: Not one piss word.

ANGELA: Tim—please.

TIM: Not one. I don't believe a gob of bile from his—

ANGELA: For my sake—please.

They embrace.

I imagine there's something I've done.

TIM: I gave him the scare of his life when he was here. We'll not see him again. He'll not be back.

ANGELA: Just because they can't have it for themselves.

TIM: Jealousy, Angela. [*He tops up his drink.*] Tomorrow's going to be a shit of a day. Until I get in the air and then… [*He drains his glass and puts it down.*] Better not have any more. I have to go in early for a roasting over my fuel bill. Then I should be able to get some leave. A couple of days, anyway. I will try and get tomorrow off.

I just have to go in for the morning. I might not be able to get the whole day off.

ANGELA: Let's go to bed.

TIM gives ANGELA *a long look then pours himself a scotch.*

TIM: Imagine you and him together. Imagine it.

ANGELA: Don't.

TIM: You'll see in the morning. In the light of day. In a couple of days or a week or so. Before you know it. Certainly before your birthday. Before the end of the year. We will all laugh about this. We will be out to dinner with friends and the whole table—including you—will fall about laughing when you recount this anecdote. It will bring the house down. You'll see. We'll be at La Terrine for the winter degustation—a table for twelve—and we'll all be laughing at—this. Before you know it. You'll see.

The telephone rings.

Let the machine get it.

ANGELA: It could be anyone.

TIM: Let the machine.

ANGELA: It could be the police.

TIM: Let the machine—

The telephone suddenly falls silent mid-ring.

We can get the number changed.

◆ ◆ ◆ ◆ ◆

SCENE THREE

ANGELA *and* TIM *and* DICK.

DICK *is wearing a fake beard and glasses.*

DICK: I'll be honest with you. James Rigby rang me last week.

TIM: Did he?

DICK: He's worried about you. And so am I.

ANGELA: James is a good friend as well as our family lawyer.

DICK: Of course he is.

TIM: We were reluctant to—at first—admittedly.

ANGELA: But he said you are exceptional at what you do.

DICK: I helped him out of a tight hole. Oh, yeah. A real bunch-up.

TIM: So you know why we need to speak to you.

DICK: I am racking my brains. But I honestly can't remember the last time I had a husband and wife team. You are married, right? Angela. Yes? Tim. Yes?

ANGELA: Yes.

DICK: I never get husband and wife together.

TIM: Well, we're both here today.

ANGELA: This is not a sordid affair being conducted in a dirty hotel room.

DICK: Not yet. Angela—your husband would have to be mentally demented to go across the road looking for romantic acceptance. When you are clearly so—how old are you? Thirty? Not older. I know skin. Are you mentally demented, Tim? I like to get these things out in the open.

TIM: Were you listening to what my wife said?

DICK: I have a tape recorder running in my pocket. I can review it later.

ANGELA: James said you had dealt with this sort of thing before.

DICK: Intimately. I bailed him out of a tight hole. A real spit and polish job. He was being targeted.

TIM: As are we.

DICK: If the cap fits.

TIM: I'm not going to call a spade an earth-inverting implement.

DICK: Shouldn't call a spade anything at all, Tim. Not in any context now. Certainly not on tape.

ANGELA: We want you to find someone for us.

DICK: There is something about you, Angela. I would love to put my finger on it.

TIM: We have had a miserable couple of weeks.

DICK: And you think I can help? I think you're right. I can.

ANGELA: Really we want to help him.

DICK: And in doing so help yourself. I believe the police are a washout.

TIM: I don't think it's at the top of their agenda.

DICK: I'm certain it's not. They have speeding fines to hand out and black kids to knock off their bikes. Only kidding. It's not their fault. Their hands are tied with red tape. The red tape needs to be cut. Angela.

ANGELA: Are you an ex-policeman?

DICK: You ever been in Basra after dark?

ANGELA: No.

DICK: Let's just leave it at that.

TIM: I've flown over it. Basra.

DICK: The Rigby Boy. James. How candid was he? Was he talking about services on the books? Or something of my more esoteric activities? When you need them.

ANGELA: He didn't specify.

DICK: Angela. Tim. Let me put you at your ease. Because before you spill your guts there are a couple of things you need to know. One— there is nothing you can tell me that I haven't already heard. If there is something that can be imagined then somewhere someone is already doing it. Probably even as we speak. And on top of that— I've already been up to my neck in it. Any filthy thing at all that you care to summon up. Children. Animals. Food. All three in one pot. And I no doubt have already put my foot in it and scraped it off. I could have thrown away the shoe—but maybe I got the smell out. Whatever it is you are mixed up in. I don't care. And I'll tell you something else. And this is vital—critical—crucial to your plight.

DICK scratches his beard as he stares around the room.

TIM: I'm sorry. No. I don't want to seem rude.

DICK: Nevertheless.

TIM: Only I have to get to the airport.

DICK: Going somewhere?

TIM: Yes.

DICK: Anywhere interesting?

TIM: Anywhere I like. I'm the pilot.

TIM laughs.

DICK: How's your fuel bill?

TIM: It's complicated.

ANGELA: Are you available to start straight away?

DICK: Eight hundred a day plus expenses and three large up front. All cash. I believe this was nutted out.

TIM: Yes. Sorry. Yes.

TIM goes into his pocket and fishes out an envelope which he gives it to DICK. DICK has a quick riffle through the envelope and then pockets it.

DICK: I imagine you feel better already. Angela.

ANGELA: Yes.

DICK: Let me tell you what I believe. I believe in good and evil. I believe in good and evil as absolutes. [*He pauses for effect.*] I like to pause for effect there.

TIM: We need you to find someone and then help us—help—them.

DICK: Help you help them with what?

ANGELA: We need to talk to them. Make them aware of all sides. And get them the help they need.

DICK: Fair enough. Don't worry about it. You should be. But don't be.

TIM: A few weeks ago—

ANGELA: It feels like a year.

DICK: A man came to your home.

TIM: He was clearly disturbed. He was talking of knowing—

DICK: In what context are we using the word knowing?

TIM: In that he knew Angela.

DICK: Knew or knew?

TIM: Knew her.

DICK: Just wanted to clarify that. Knew.

ANGELA: I didn't.

DICK: And you let him in?

TIM: I take people on their word. I believe innocent until proven.

DICK: And what do you think now?

TIM: What do I think?

DICK: About the whole benefit of the doubt thing. See, I think it's part of a bygone age. By all means think of it nostalgically. But don't ever act like it still means something.

ANGELA: We had no reason to suspect anything. Nor would we want to.

DICK: And what do you think now? A man comes to your door. I know so and so. And you say come in and have a drink I'll give gorgeous a shout—she's just in the shower. Were you in the shower, Angela?

ANGELA: I was in the garden.

DICK: Dirty hands. Green fingers.

ANGELA: I was taking some cuttings.

DICK: Did you wipe your hands on your top or on your thighs?

TIM: I am not going to be scared to open my front door to someone.

DICK: And you shouldn't be. Don't lock it. Leave it open. I do. I hope someone uninvited does come in. I've gone years and never had a knock. Some people go a whole lifetime and only find goodwill and charity. Others—not. That's the nature of good and evil. It doesn't look any different—not anymore. Villains don't have beards and capes and robes and speak with funny voices. Some do. Admittedly. Let me guess. He was white. Clean. Well spoken. Smartly dressed. All boxes ticked.

TIM: He knew Angela by name.

DICK: Shit. No, it's fine.

TIM: He knew where she lived and where she worked.

ANGELA: We had no reason to expect someone was targeting us.

DICK: No guilty conscience? 'Course not. And I would have let him in as well. But I clearly don't have what he wants. Fortunately. What does he want?

TIM: It's difficult to say.

DICK: Angela? Any thoughts?

ANGELA: We fear what he could do without the proper care.

DICK: You're not alone.

TIM: He wanted to be in our house. In our faces.

DICK: Did you bash him?

ANGELA: Did I bash him?

DICK: Either of you?

TIM: No.

ANGELA: Definitely not.

DICK: But you threatened him with a tasting plate.

TIM: He said he would see us again. He would be where we couldn't look away. He said enjoy your stuff while it lasts. He said dance, selfish—fuckers.

DICK: Verbatim? Now that shits me. That's a reference made just to disturb you. I can't be doing with these shit-pot amateur psychologists. They're the most dangerous.

ANGELA: It could be nothing.

DICK: No. It's something. It's something all right. Don't panic—yet.

ANGELA: Of course not.

DICK: But thank Christ you called me. Seriously. This is part of a bigger deadly pattern.

ANGELA: We are not vindictive people, Dick. We want to help him.

DICK: You still have the right to feel safe about your own home.

TIM: I think that it is something that as a civilised people—

DICK: No.

TIM: No? Sorry?

DICK: The whole civilised people thing. It's too long a bow.

ANGELA: Is there anything you can do?

DICK: Are you outraged? How would you describe it? Are you outraged? Would you go that far? Are you up for the fight?

ANGELA: We are not looking for a fight. The opposite.

DICK: Fight. Fight. And the police are a washout. It's not their fault. They need more powers. They're getting them. But not quick enough. They do what they can. And you did the right thing. And not a moment too soon.

TIM: You need to understand—my wife needs to stay completely relaxed. Do you understand? Completely calm. That's the point of us being here. We need that calm space that comes with knowing something is fixed.

ANGELA: I've recently found out I am some point in my first trimester.

> TIM *takes* ANGELA *by the hand.*

DICK: Some point?

ANGELA: And we have been trying for such a very long time.

TIM: Angela—

ANGELA: I'm explaining how important this is. And why we would come to this.

DICK: Been trying for such a very long time. Just making notes.

ANGELA: We had given up really.

DICK: Given up.

ANGELA: We had stopped trying.

TIM: Seriously, darling—

DICK: Don't apologise, Tim.

ANGELA: What I am saying is this pregnancy is so—so important for us.

DICK: When you had given up trying.

TIM: It's very complicated.

DICK: Like your fuel bill.

ANGELA: What is important—there is a high risk—associated—with my history.

DICK: Gynaecologists. They'd eat their dinner through the letter box if you'd let them. Stress is the last thing you need.

ANGELA: Yes.

TIM: So this torment has to stop. This not knowing—

ANGELA: It's the not knowing that is so excruciating.

TIM: It has to stop. And now. Right now. Please.

ANGELA *and* TIM *wait for* DICK *to respond.*

DICK: What are you staring at?

TIM: We were explaining about how important this has become.

DICK: Yeah. But you were staring at something.

TIM: I didn't realise I was. I'm sure I wasn't.

ANGELA: I don't think you were, darling.

DICK: You were staring at something.

TIM: If I was—

DICK: You were staring at my beard.

TIM: I don't think so.

ANGELA: Are you asking us if it suits you?

TIM: I really don't think I was staring.

ANGELA: Some men can wear a beard.

DICK: Touch it.

ANGELA: No thank you.

DICK: Touch it. What strikes you about it?

TIM: Absolutely nothing significant.

DICK: It's fake. You picked it.

TIM: I can't say that I did.

ANGELA: I didn't.

DICK: My number one beard is getting washed.

ANGELA: Yes.

DICK: This is my stand-in. Feel it. It's nylon.

TIM: I truly didn't notice.

DICK: I only use this one for long work. Or on a job which is quick in and out. I fit you in today as a special favour to your pal Rigby.

ANGELA: And we are very grateful.

DICK: Just means I haven't had chance to take the second-choice tickler off. Don't let the fact you picked it rattle your confidence in me.

ANGELA: It hasn't. And we didn't.

TIM: I didn't even notice it.

DICK: And you're desperate.

ANGELA: Yes.

TIM: I wouldn't say that.

DICK: No. You're desperate. And I get my first-choice beard back on Monday anyway so everything's...

ANGELA: We've written down a description.

DICK: This is recalled from three weeks ago?

TIM: Yes.

DICK: It's not worth the paper it's written on. What else have you got?

TIM: We have had a number of phone calls that just stop ringing before they're answered.

ANGELA: We did the dial-back thing and they are mostly silent numbers.

DICK: What's being done about that?

TIM: Our service provider is looking into it.

DICK: Those bastards will do nothing. You probably spoke to some out-of-work actor. Soon as you hung up it would have gone in the bin.

ANGELA: We did get a real number twice.

DICK: What did you do?

TIM: We rang it.

DICK: Holy shit. Don't ever—don't—don't do that.

ANGELA: Turns out it's a public telephone.

TIM: And we know where.

DICK: Is it on the sheet?

ANGELA: Everything is written there for you.

> DICK *casts an eye over the papers.*

DICK: You've had underwear go missing.

TIM: Yes.

DICK: Angela.

ANGELA: Yes.

DICK: Silk? I can't imagine you tolerating anything else.

ANGELA: Silk. Yes.

DICK: You don't have them, do you?

TIM: Me?

DICK: You think it's impossible?

ANGELA: Also somebody collected dry cleaning that was in my name. Someone who fits his description.

DICK: What colour?

ANGELA: It was a brown coat.

DICK: No. The scanties.

TIM: Is it really important?

DICK: Do you think I can haul this filth of a bloke in and you still keep your precious privacy? What colour?

ANGELA: Two black and one—aquamarine.

DICK: Two black. One—you sure it was aquamarine? Couldn't be topaz. Like an ocean blue?

TIM: My wife is an interior designer.

DICK: What genre of pieces are we talking about?

TIM: Is this absolutely necessary?

DICK: You got something to hide?

TIM: No.

DICK: Then what are you afraid of?

TIM: That this maniac is capable of—anything. And he wants us to know it.

DICK: We don't have much to go on. What if he's been trying to sell them?

ANGELA: Secondhand underwear?

DICK: Believe me, there is a market for everything and anything out there. You should see some of the things I've bought.

ANGELA: A bra and two g-strings.

DICK: He won't have sold them. He'll have them very close—as much as it turns my guts to say it. And this bloke is a sick fucking—excuse me but—he's torturing you remotely with his shit-pot amateur psychology. Don't give in to him. You're stronger than that. I can see that just from your skin.

ANGELA: Thank you.

DICK: Cup size on the bra?

TIM: No. I'm sorry.

DICK: Yes Tim?

TIM: No. I'm serious now. If you can't see that my wife is distressed enough then I'm sorry but no. When we have already explained—

DICK: I can see she's distressed. And I am aware of her condition. Don't apologise, Tim.

TIM: Quite frankly, you seem to be—seem to be—

DICK: I seem to be what?

TIM: We have had this month of crank phone calls. A month of not knowing what he is capable of. We have had things going missing. Our post has been opened.

DICK: This is why you need me. Don't panic. But I have seen this torture before. It always escalates.

TIM: Imagine what it has been like for my wife. She has to go to people's houses—people she has never met.

DICK: And you away for days on end—imagining what might be possible. It's horrifying.

TIM: We have on a number of occasions found letters that are open or half open. We are convinced that small things have been moved around our house.

DICK: I'm writing this down.

ANGELA: Which means he has been in our house.

DICK: Could be your cleaner?

TIM: No.

DICK: Very close to her, are you?

ANGELA: We don't have one at the moment. I'm working from home—temporarily.

TIM: I know these are only small things that have happened. But they accumulate. And the feelings—our feelings—

DICK: Small things accumulate—go on.

TIM: This is serious.

DICK: It is serious. And I don't want her stressed any more than you, mate.

ANGELA: And I've seen him. I've seen him twice for absolute certain.

TIM: It's getting so Angela can't answer the phone.

DICK: Interior design?

ANGELA: That's right.

DICK: What if it's an emergency?

TIM: He was cleaning windscreens at an intersection. He grinned at me. I was going to get out and brain him.

DICK: Don't brain him.

ANGELA: He wouldn't brain him.

DICK: I do the braining now. I love a bit of brain.

TIM: The lights changed. When I turned he was gone.

DICK: And you see him everywhere.

ANGELA: I can see what you are thinking.

DICK: No you can't.

ANGELA: I get a sense of what you are thinking.

DICK: You really don't.

ANGELA: He sent me an email.

TIM: He sent you an email and you didn't say?

ANGELA: On my work email.

TIM: Why didn't you say?

ANGELA: You're already so stressed—about me. Which makes me more stressed. And we had already agreed to do something so—

DICK: Return address?

ANGELA: Yes. An address anyway.

TIM: What was in the email? What did he say?

ANGELA: Absolutely noting at all.

DICK: This burns me. This shit-pot amateur psychology is becoming epidemic. He left it blank so you had to fill it with your imagination. He's a cruel fucker. Excuse me, but there is nothing worse than the contents of your own head. Room 101. You know your darkest private-most filthiest fears. Leave a blank space and in they pour like spew. If you want to know what you are capable of—look at a blank space. That's why I have so many pictures.

TIM: So what do you suggest?

DICK: You two are in deep shit. You don't need me to tell you that. [*To* ANGELA] You probably need someone to hold you.

TIM: I've used up all my leave at work.

ANGELA: We want him found and helped.

DICK: Stopped.

TIM: We said helped.

DICK: And I said stopped. Which is it?

ANGELA: You must understand.

DICK: I do.

TIM: I don't think you do.

DICK: Do you want me to find this disease and cure it? Or do you want me to polish your shoes, Captain?

TIM: I understand violent men.

DICK: Okay.

TIM: I broke a man's nose once.

DICK: On the rugby field with the old-boys' fifteen.

TIM: How did you know?

DICK: What do I do for a living?

ANGELA: We want him stopped.

DICK: What did Rigby tell you about me? Did he say I was the best? Did he say I am the only man to get the job done or not? Did he say I am the sweet antidote to tension and misery or not?

ANGELA: We want him stopped, yes. But you have to understand what we are saying.

DICK: I do. Believe me, I do. You want him stopped. I am the best. And you want him stopped.

ANGELA: Yes.

TIM: [*with* ANGELA] Yes.

ANGELA: By definition.

TIM: Yes.

DICK: Then look no further. Dick is the answer.

◆ ◆ ◆ ◆ ◆

SCENE FOUR

DICK.

DICK *removes his fake beard and glasses.*

DICK: Don't get me started on the level of hygiene in the majority of public toilets. You try applying the tools of the trade under a blue fluoro-light. I remember a time when you didn't need safe needle disposal for taking a shit. But there you go. There's nothing funny anymore. Everything's gone beyond laughter. It's open slather out there. I'll give you the précis. Number one rule for happy living—be true to yourself. No one else is going to be. And that way—at least you'll know you're the real deal. Even if no one else does. I read all the magazines. I have a lot of time on my hands. That's part and parcel of my caper. [*As he speaks he applies a fake moustache and a hairpiece.*] A mate of mine had a trap for catching crows. Because he hated them. I was round there one day and he had a crow on a bit of fishing line and it was flying round and round. Squawk. It was amazing how quick the thrill of it died off. And he just took the fishing line and smashed the bird against the wall. Birds kind of explode. I was only ten. And I said I've got to go home. And he said you just got here. It was hard to go but I thought if I stayed he might smash me against a wall. [*He considers his façade then continues.*] That was the first time I ever saw my mum in the raw. I got home and went to find mum. Just to get a drink or money or something. And there she was—buff. Birthday suit. In the raw. In the middle of the day. During school holidays. I never asked her why. Never mentioned it. But I got more lollies and red drink those school holidays than any other before—after or since. [*He puts the finishing touches to his façade. Focussing on an imaginary friend*] I imagine you spend quite a bit of time here on your own. With your husband away—with his job. Are you here on your own quite a lot? I imagine you are. Look at the state of this place. Look what this filth has done. Did the police dab the place for prints? [*He waits for a reply.*] Do you believe a person could love a person—really love a person—after they'd only met them—once?

◆◆◆◆◆

SCENE FIVE

TIM *and* DEZ.

DEZ *is eating a doughnut.*

DEZ: This is awkward.

TIM: You need to know I have called security. They will be here any second.

DEZ: I like to come here and watch the planes take off and land.

TIM: You should also know I have engaged a detective.

DEZ: Congratulations. Do you think it will be a long engagement? [*He laughs.*] Are you a pilot?

TIM: I am really out of patience with you. You see that camera? Do you see that camera? That is the reason why I haven't descended on you.

DEZ: I used to come here as a kid.

TIM: Once the detective has your details he will pass them on to the authorities.

DEZ: Do you want to know where I live?

TIM: You're enjoying this, aren't you? You really are as sick as he says. My wife—

DEZ: Angela.

TIM: —wants to put you in a private facility. Personally I would like to stand on your throat.

DEZ: How is Angela?

TIM: Fuck you. I'm sorry. But fuck you.

DEZ: Which is your plane?

TIM: Say that again. Make a statement like that. You will spend two weeks locked up just for breathing out. Which is my plane? Why? Fuck you. Why?

DEZ: I was just going to keep an eye out for you taking off.

TIM: For the love of God, please. For the love of God. You have religion.

DEZ: I'm lapsed.

TIM: Think what you are doing to Angela. She needs—she doesn't need—leave us alone.

DEZ: Is she well?

TIM: She needs you to leave her alone.

DEZ: Sure.

TIM: Please. I don't know your agenda. I don't know your purpose. But please, for the love of God—just leave us alone.

DEZ: Okay.

TIM: Please. I am appealing to you as another human being.

DEZ: What time does you flight leave?

TIM: You are a sick putrid twisted—do something criminal so you can be hauled in. Ask me again which is my plane. Ask me what time my flight leaves. I will have security stick their fingers so far up your arse your gums will bleed. You come here just as I am about to—and ask—and stand there knowing I am outbound. Security will seriously finger-fuck you. When they get here.

DEZ: They're probably detained somewhere reading their workplace agreements.

TIM: Why are you doing this to us? Why us?

DEZ: Tim—

TIM: We will see how you like it. How do you think you will like it?

DEZ: Tim—

TIM: Have you done something to my—?

DEZ: Tim. You're a pilot. I like aeroplanes. That's all this is.

TIM: I know what you're doing. You think I'm stupid. You think I don't know that you will go right up to the boundary of law. I am telling you. I am making this statement as clearly as I possibly can. If Angela sees you once more—once more—I think you know what I am capable of.

DEZ: I think what you just said is criminal, Tim. That statement.

TIM: Let me worry about that.

DEZ: Will they be able to pick up the movement of your lips on the cameras?

TIM: Do you have a human bone in your body?

DEZ: I know you have a good lawyer. But don't threaten people with 'whatever it is you are capable of'. Not when you are about to fly a plane across the Bay of Bengal.

TIM: What do you know of my flight path?

DEZ: You don't want to be late.

TIM: You cocksucker. You lousy fucking cocksucker. I am calling the police this instant.

DEZ: I'm not going anywhere. Tell them I'm right here. I'm just standing here watching the planes take off and land.

TIM: Please. Why? Why? You are the foulest fucking mess. Why? What is it you want? Let her be. She needs to be—man to man—Mate. Mate. Mate. Whatever it is you think. Promise me—promise me you won't go near her any more.

DEZ: Okay. I won't.

TIM: You foul fucking pernicious stinking flagrant fucking rat cunt.

◆ ◆ ◆ ◆ ◆

SCENE SIX

DICK *and* ANGELA.

DICK *wears a fake moustache and hairpiece.* ANGELA *is tidying up a smashed vase/ornament.*

DICK: You have the most beautiful surfaces. Yes. We are deep in the domain of French-polish here. And it's quite an art when you get it done right. I imagine you spend quite a bit of time here on your own. With your husband—away with his job. And you're here on your own with nothing but your thoughts. Look at the state of this place. Look what this filth has done. Did the police dab the place for prints?

ANGELA: Yes.

DICK: It is the worst feeling. The most filthy intrusion. To know that someone has been here—amongst it—in your stuff.

ANGELA: This is not the first time.

DICK: That's true.

ANGELA: It wasn't so violent last time.

DICK: These things do escalate.

ANGELA: I was out for perhaps an hour.

DICK: Came back and found things turned over.

ANGELA: Yes.

DICK: They'll find no fingerprints. He's too cute for that. Anything get taken?

ANGELA: I don't know yet.

DICK: There won't be. This is the piss-pot amateur psychology I was talking about. You're flushed. Look at your skin. Is it hot to the touch?

ANGELA: I'm pissed off. Thoroughly pissed off.

DICK: And hormonal as all hell, I bet. But you're holding it together. You look—

ANGELA: I am really sick of this feeling.

DICK: And you should be.

ANGELA: I didn't think it could get any worse.

DICK: I think all things considered you are—fantastic.

　　DICK *looks the place over.*

ANGELA: You said you had some news.

DICK: Yes I did.

ANGELA: Is it something that the authorities can use?

DICK: Are you taking any pills?

ANGELA: Am I taking pills?

DICK: For your nerves.

ANGELA: I can't take pills.

DICK: Can't swallow. You're going to have a natural birth, then?

ANGELA: You said there was some news.

DICK: Were you crying? On the phone.

ANGELA: I was very upset.

DICK: I was surprised you answered.

ANGELA: I'm not completely paralysed with fear.

DICK: Yeah. Maybe you should be. Maybe you shouldn't answer the phone. Not until—

ANGELA: Until when?

DICK: Until I give the all clear. Natural birth, eh. Ever heard of the birth-orgasm?

ANGELA: No.

DICK: It exists. I was reading about it. Most western women don't experience it because they take drugs—painkillers, yeah. Apparently it's the biggest ever. There's this knot of nerve endings really has no other purpose. And when the baby's head exerts pressure in the sweet spot… I've been having an extended look at your home security.

ANGELA: How is it?

> ANGELA *laughs.*

DICK: How are you holding up?

ANGELA: As well as can be expected.

DICK: You look amazing. And you've never heard of it—the birth-orgasm?

ANGELA: My home has been broken into.

DICK: I have had weeks scouring this filthy city.

ANGELA: I don't sit here in the dark afraid to move.

DICK: I've been passed now and then. I've had a good look. [*He takes his mobile phone out and cues up a photograph.*] I took a picture.

ANGELA: Of the house?

DICK: No.

ANGELA: You took a picture. You took a picture? Of what?

DICK: Of a man. Paparazzo style.

ANGELA: A man. You've found him?

DICK: Don't know.

ANGELA: I can't believe you've found him. You've found him.

DICK: I don't know I have. You tell me.

> *He holds the camera out for her. She looks at it.*

He didn't see me. He was too busy browsing the army surplus. [*He looks at the camera.*] Sorry. Shit. Sorry. Not that one. I'm sorry. That's the wrong one. [*He leaves the camera at arm's length.*] I suppose you're offended now. By this picture and its content.

ANGELA: No.

DICK: I have to take pictures as necessary, you see. Of all nature of things—

ANGELA: I'm not offended.

DICK: I don't know if you'd call that nature or not. You weren't supposed to see that.

ANGELA: It's fine.

DICK: It didn't upset you?

ANGELA: It's fine.

DICK: You weren't offended?

ANGELA: No.

DICK: You're an amazing woman.

ANGELA: If you have a photograph I would like to see it. And now, please. Please.

DICK: Another one in this sequence? Yeah. I reckon you can work out how this story ends.

He cues up another photo on his phone. He holds out the camera for ANGELA *to look at. She looks then she moves away.*

That's him, then?

ANGELA: Yes.

DICK: Shit. You sure?

ANGELA: That's him.

DICK: Shifty-looking prick, isn't he? He is a nasty-looking piece of work. And it's definitely him?

ANGELA: I don't know how many times you want me to tell you yes.

DICK: Shit. Shit.

ANGELA: Has something bad happened?

DICK: Look around you.

ANGELA: Apart from this invasion of—

DICK: Something bad happened when you did the ID on this mongrel. Shit.

ANGELA: Have you spoken to him?

DICK: I was hoping I wouldn't have to. Shit.

ANGELA: But you were trying to find him for that express reason.

DICK: I was hoping it wasn't him. Shit. Well, it is him. Okay. Shit. Okay. No, that's fine. Shit.

ANGELA: So you will speak to him? Now that you've found him. Explain what all this is doing to us. Help him get care. Find out if he has an alibi.

DICK: You need dabs. You need rational motive. You need a witness. He'll have an alibi.

ANGELA: Then what? What the hell is going to be done?

DICK: Shit. Okay. No, that's fine. Shit.

ANGELA: We need to get him—us—some—care.

DICK: That's a fact.

ANGELA: Where is he?

DICK: I don't know.

ANGELA: But you have a picture.

DICK: That's all I have. He didn't go anywhere. He just walked around all night.

He browses the photos on his mobile.

ANGELA: Will you be able find where he's living?

DICK: I bet he's living in a hole in the ground. Burrowed up to his neck with army surplus and tins of beans and jars of mince. I'll find his lair—given time and money.

ANGELA: A friend of mine is a clinical psychologist.

DICK: I bet that costs.

ANGELA: She was telling me that there is this—a facility. She believes she can get him admitted past the waiting list.

DICK: I'll to have to get his specific whereabouts first.

ANGELA: Money is not an issue.

DICK: God, would I love to say that.

ANGELA: I simply meant—

DICK: Don't apologise for doing well.

ANGELA: I'm not.

DICK: Don't feel guilty.

ANGELA: I don't.

DICK: But you want him sectioned.

ANGELA: This is a private facility.

DICK: I hope I never upset you. [*He straightens his moustache.*] I found him. I found him. Are you impressed?

ANGELA: I want to know what is being done?

DICK: This bloke. He's not upset. He's not got self-esteem issues. He didn't fall out with his dad when he got caught fiddling under the doona. This bloke is rabid. You are not to go near him. You or anyone hasn't had their shots. The powers that be are moving like treacle. I've seen mould move quicker. Look at me, Angela. Look at me. I have never been more serious. When I have him pinned down—if you try and put him in a facility he will go feral. You don't have the right to have him sectioned—and neither does your doctor and she knows it. But if you try he will go—ballistic. Game over.

ANGELA *looks at him.*

I'm going to make everything bad good again. I can. I am the man of the moment. I'm going to make it all go away.

ANGELA: Dick is the answer.

DICK: I ran his photo through a friend of mine who has access to the necessary records. You should have seen us. Grown men do weep. I've put his bribe down on the expenses as massage therapy.

ANGELA: Did he appear on the database?

DICK: High and handsome.

ANGELA: So he has a criminal record?

DICK: He's way too cute for that.

ANGELA: So now you can pass his whereabouts on when you have them.

DICK: Sure. But what happens between then and the six months it takes to process his file through the various levels of management? I'm worried, Angela. No. That's not true. I'm scared. Probably shouldn't tell you that. But there you are. I'm scared of what could and might—will happen. What's this—? Not even a burglary. It's a sick mind at work.

ANGELA: But if they know what he is capable of.

DICK: Suspicions, yeah. What are they? Take them to the International Court.

ANGELA: But he has done something.

DICK: Shit-pot remote psychological torture. They'd never pin that on him. He's too good for that. Too cute. He wouldn't risk getting pinched until he was going for the endgame. And he's not up to that yet. And when he does… I looked at his files. You think mercury is

slippery. [*He looks at a photo on his phone and then puts it away.*]
Do you believe in prevention or cure, Angela?

ANGELA: Both. Prevention.

DICK: See—here is where law and medicine part company. Law is
deterrent and punishment. It doesn't work. Because this is disease.
We need to treat it like a disease because that is what it is. And we
need to think like disease to cure it. I've had a disease. We need
to fight fire with fire. We need to do anything and everything the
disease would do without thought or concern for morals and dinner
party indignation and shame. You remember I said I believe in good
and evil as absolute?

ANGELA: Yes. I don't agree.

DICK: I'm not saying it's his fault. I'm not portioning out blame. But
nevertheless he is evil.

ANGELA: Ill?

DICK: He's never been certified—which really only proves the pressure
the health system is under. [*He adjusts his hair.*] Angela. I am going
to stay here tonight.

ANGELA: No.

DICK: I'll bed down here.

ANGELA: I'll be fine.

DICK: No you won't. So I'll stay here.

ANGELA: I'll be fine.

DICK: I should stay here tonight. I'll stay here.

ANGELA: I will get a friend to stay with me.

DICK: I am a friend. We'll bed down.

ANGELA: I don't think you should stay here.

DICK: Is Tim coming back tonight?

ANGELA: Yes.

DICK: You know there are at least seven indicators of a lie. I counted
five.

ANGELA: I want to know what it is you suggest. What it is you intend
to do. What it is you advise we can do.

DICK: Hey. Angela. Hey. Calm down. This is what he wants. Calm
down. For the baby's sake.

ANGELA: If he knew me he would not do this. He thinks he knows me
but he doesn't. I know things are—wrong and I do what I can to
change them.

DICK: Very difficult to bring about societal change with a mortgage this big.

ANGELA: He would not do this if he knew me.

DICK: He doesn't want to know you. He wants to hurt you. Because you are beautiful. Because you are the cream. What is the point of hurting ugly shit? That happens every day and who hears about that? He wants to hurt you because you are an anonymous but beautiful personification of the cream of the milk coming out of the dominant teat of power. [*He tries to get a drink out of the dregs of an empty glass.*] Let me try and explain that again. It didn't come out right. What he is doing—it's not political, it's about who he is—beyond talk and chatter and long lunches and left or right.

ANGELA: It's about teats.

DICK: That didn't come out right.

ANGELA: You know skin.

DICK: Exactly. Skin. Look at you. And I should stay here tonight. Because you need someone to hold you.

ANGELA: You will not stay here tonight.

DICK: You would enjoy it. Try it on.

ANGELA: I will go to a hotel.

DICK: Stay here. Don't be driven out of your home. Bring a bottle of something in here and we can nut out a plan.

ANGELA: No.

DICK: Yeah. We'll nut something out together.

ANGELA: I don't want to.

DICK: We'll grab a bottle and lock up and cosy down and nut something out. Come on. Give it a squeeze. Just try it on for size.

ANGELA: Get out. Get away from me.

DICK: Get on board.

ANGELA: Go away.

DICK: I'm helping you.

ANGELA: This is helping?

DICK: Do you believe a person could deeply love a person—truly love a person—after they'd only met them once?

ANGELA: Get the fuck out of my house.

DICK: You ever rung a psychic hotline?

ANGELA: Get the fuck out of my house.

DICK *waits for more.*

DICK: Ten thousand. Ten thousand cash and all it goes away. Don't ask. Ten thousand and a quick look away. Look the other way. Ten large. It's not a matter of money. So don't ask. Don't know. Just give me the folding. And get on with your life. I can make it all go away. I can make everything bad disappear. What do you want me to do? Just what the fuck do you want me to do? Think about it. I know skin. Mum. Mum. I'm bleeding, Mum. It all ends up the same. And I am not going anywhere—not until—see, you need to decide. You need someone to hold you so tight. And you know it. Why can't you admit it? Ten thousand cash and it all goes away. Any thoughts?

◆ ◆ ◆ ◆ ◆

SCENE SEVEN

ANGELA *and* TIM.

TIM *has a tumbler of scotch.*

TIM: I think we should stay in a hotel. I feel pathetic. Useless. I think we should get a furnished apartment.
ANGELA: For how long?
TIM: Until whenever.
ANGELA: That is what I am asking.
TIM: Then I don't know.
ANGELA: Me neither.
TIM: I'm drinking too much. This bottle is almost gone.
ANGELA: I didn't drink it.
TIM: I wouldn't blame you if you had. I think of you here on your own— [*He drinks.*] You look fabulous.
ANGELA: Thank you.
TIM: I feel like shit. I miss you.
ANGELA: Everything's fine.
TIM: That is what I should say. But everything is not fine. And yet there is fuck-all I can do. How does that make me feel? [*He drinks.*] We should go to a hotel. Order room service. [*He drinks.*] This is—I am—it's like a cruel joke. Impotent is not the word. [*He sips his drink.*] I've been suspended, darling.

ANGELA: I know.

TIM: It was very hard for me to tell you.

ANGELA: I said how sorry I was.

TIM: I have been suspended. I feel thoroughly disgraced to have to tell you that on top of all this. But I have. [*He drinks.*] Suspended pending psych assessment. [*He laughs then sips his drink.*] Yes. I think about you a lot.

ANGELA: I thought the thing about your fuel costs had been—

TIM: Justified? Yes. I just fly balls first into black and grey regardless now. Yes. No fuel concerns now.

ANGELA: But you made a joke?

TIM: I made a joke.

ANGELA: And they suspended you?

TIM: Pending psych. Would you like to hear the joke?

ANGELA: There is no joke that should get you suspended.

TIM: It was more of a wry comment. An observation. I made an observation to my first officer. And my first officer felt compelled to pass it on. Cunt. And now I am grounded. Indefinitely.

ANGELA: Pending psych?

TIM: And what the fuck does that mean? I'm sorry. But what the fuck does that mean?

> ANGELA *touches him on the arm.*

I'm a good pilot. I'm a good person.

ANGELA: You are.

TIM: I made one lousy tongue-in-cheek observation and now I am unfit. There is nobody who cares more for his passengers than me. Self-loading cargo they are called. Not by me. They are people. And I am not unfit.

ANGELA: What did you say that made them suspend you?

TIM: We were over Kabul. Not over—southwest. And I simply said—I asked—how do you feel about turning northeast and crashing this oily bird into Kabul Central? Such as it is. Drop twelve hundred tonnes of burning oil on Main Street Kabul? How do you feel about going into the history books as the men who pointed the finger of absurdity at the slimy shit we do to each other? For petrol. Then I laughed. Only joking, I said. And laughed. Just occurred to me, I said. A passing thought. And laughed. And so we went on. A good tailwind. A little bit of bounce over the Bay of Bengal and then smooth and clear the rest of the way. Bit of a queue at Heathrow.

ANGELA: You didn't mean it.

TIM: It was a question. The question was serious, yes. I wasn't saying do it. But I was seriously asking. Yes. Do you think I'm mental? [*He laughs.*] Have you ever been in a room with people—your superiors—clearly thinking you are mental? Miserable. And now I bring it in here with you. After this—vile intrusion.

ANGELA: I don't think you are.

TIM: Thank you.

ANGELA: I think I am.

TIM: No.

ANGELA: I think I am.

TIM: There is nothing about you that could be considered—let me get the right word.

> TIM *searches for the right word.*

ANGELA: I crashed the car, Tim.

TIM: You crashed the car?

ANGELA: It's funny. With everything. I crashed the car. I'm sorry.

TIM: You're not hurt. Tell me you're not.

ANGELA: I'm not. I'm fine.

TIM: You're fine.

ANGELA: Yes. And I'm sorry.

TIM: You're fine. Tell me you are—

ANGELA: It could have been so much worse. But yes—I'm fine.

TIM: It was just a prang? A bump?

ANGELA: I didn't want to tell you. It's in the garage.

TIM: On top of everything. You gave the car a—prang. We're getting a hotel tonight. That's for damn sure.

ANGELA: Then tomorrow?

TIM: We will sleep tonight.

ANGELA: I nearly hit a woman with a pram.

TIM: Angela—

ANGELA: I went up the kerb. But everyone is fine. Everyone is so fine it makes me want to scream.

TIM: Did a dog run out? A brick in the road? A dead bird?

ANGELA: A car was following me.

TIM: A car was following you.

ANGELA: A car was following me.

TIM: So you were preoccupied with the rear-view mirror.

ANGELA: It was—

TIM: And you are in one piece.

ANGELA: I ran up the pavement. People were walking. It was a school zone. She had a pram.

TIM: But you're unhurt.

ANGELA: I nearly killed her, Tim.

TIM: But you didn't. It's funny. You and the car and me and my plane. But you didn't. I didn't. [*He laughs and drains his glass.*] Did you go and talk to Tony?

ANGELA: I went straight to Tony and had a full check-up.

TIM: If I could get my hands on the bastard I would—not our doctor. Not Tony. Tony is a good doctor.

ANGELA: What would you do?

TIM: Me?

ANGELA: If you could get your hands on him? What would you do?

TIM: Get the old boys' rugby fifteen together and stand on his head for an hour.

ANGELA: Yes.

TIM: You're not hurt. I'm sorry I wasn't more sympathetic. No I am. I wasn't thinking. You've been in a car accident and all I care about is my suspension. I am not unfit. And you went and saw Tony?

ANGELA: Yes.

TIM: And what did he say?

ANGELA: He's a little worried.

TIM: He's worried?

ANGELA: Not worried.

TIM: Did he prescribe something?

ANGELA: More tests.

TIM: Isn't there a pill? A pill of some kind. A pill that will—

ANGELA: I don't want a pill.

TIM: No. Why should you? No. I'm just thinking breathing space. That's all. A few tests—that's all. And how do you feel—in yourself?

ANGELA: Like misery walked over my grave.

ANGELA *laughs.*

TIM: Not worried—concerned. No pills, just rest.

ANGELA: He wants me to go in and see him every day.

TIM: Yes. Well. Then. Fuck it. Fuck it. They've only gone and suspended me over a fucking shit joke—comment—about—nothing. The miserable shit bastards. I seriously mean—fuck them all. And I am away for three days and it kills me to leave you here alone. I hate it. And now. And now I come back and you have crashed the car because you believe—because you were—I believe you were being followed. And you have—I have—I had absolutely no intention of doing the thing. And the house has been—what is even the right word? Polluted. And there is nothing I can do. And I want to do something. I wanted to love the idea that we would never need that prick Dick again. Fuck it, Angela. But look at this. Look at us. Fuck it all. I love you, Angela. Fuck this. I love you. You are so beautiful. I love you. And me—I am—

He goes to drink but his glass is empty.

ANGELA: He's found him.

TIM: He's found him?

ANGELA: Yesterday. He's seen him. He took a picture.

TIM: Yesterday.

ANGELA: He is following him.

TIM: And then when he corners him—

ANGELA: And for ten thousand dollars it will all stop forever, immediately.

TIM: Ten thousand?

ANGELA: That's all.

TIM: It's not much.

ANGELA: Not much. No.

TIM: You'd think that it would cost more.

ANGELA: Are you thinking about it?

TIM: I'm thinking about it. But I am not thinking about it.

ANGELA: No.

TIM: No.

ANGELA: Not that I don't hate things the way they are.

TIM: Look at me. Look what it has come to for me. Ask me if I hate things the way they are?

ANGELA: I know you do.

TIM: You nearly killed a woman. And that would have been your fault. But it wasn't your fault. We are good people.

ANGELA: We are good people. That's the point.

TIM: This is—this must be miserable for you.

ANGELA: It's really appalling to feel the way I do. That also is the point.

TIM: Ten thousand.

ANGELA: Ten thousand.

TIM: It's not much, is it?

ANGELA: No.

TIM: Of course we can't do it. I know that. I'm merely saying.

ANGELA: I know.

TIM: Imagine if we had read in the paper—a mystery man was found in the harbour. We had never met him, never heard of him. But now if someone turns up in a river all of a sudden it would be a massive issue.

ANGELA: If you give someone ten thousand—

TIM: I don't suppose we would hear anything at all. I suppose that is the point. Do you suppose that is what James had in mind when he put us on to him?

ANGELA: I haven't asked him.

TIM: And don't. The less people who know the better. Don't implicate anyone. Least of all James.

ANGELA: I haven't told anyone.

TIM: Don't mention it to anyone. Not that we are going to do anything, but don't mention it anyway.

ANGELA: I won't mention it to anyone. I don't want anyone else to know.

TIM: To anyone. Anyone at all.

ANGELA: This is just between us.

TIM *laughs.*

TIM: What an absurd—what a thoroughly absurd disgusting situation to find yourself in.

ANGELA: It's appalling. It's absolutely disgusting.

TIM: It is the most vile—I mean—is there ever truly a right answer?

ANGELA: Not that I know.

TIM: No. There is no right answer, is there? Not anymore.

ANGELA: I don't think so.

TIM: I mean what is the right thing to do? Crash the car and kill a mother and child? Drop twelve hundred tonnes on Kabul? Twelve hundred tonnes. Four hundred souls. Or cough up ten grand and have a—life—a life of sorts.

ANGELA: Are you seriously thinking about it?

TIM: I don't know.

ANGELA: No. Good.

TIM: No.

ANGELA: Don't.

TIM: I am seriously thinking about it. Doesn't mean I am seriously thinking—

ANGELA: Good.

TIM: No.

ANGELA: No. Good.

TIM: But you have to ask the question.

ANGELA: This is a—what is this—a discussion?

TIM: Our feelings and our experience are in conflict with our ideology. Perhaps ideology has to go. [*He laughs.*] We didn't ask to be targeted. We didn't invite this.

ANGELA: Didn't we?

TIM: We did not.

ANGELA: I agree. I'm just asking.

TIM: I imagine he is waiting for a decision of some sort.

ANGELA: Yes.

TIM: Sitting in his car somewhere anonymous.

ANGELA: I can picture it.

TIM: I suppose he has left a number where we can reach him twenty-four hours a day.

ANGELA: He has.

TIM: And what do you think? No, seriously. What do you think? No. Forget I asked. Don't give it another thought. Forget it. But what do you really think? And I am talking from the pit of my heart. Look that deep. From the very—from that thing—the very pit of my heart. What do you really think?

ANGELA: More than anything. What I want now. I want a family.

◆ ◆ ◆ ◆ ◆

SCENE EIGHT

DICK *and* DEZ.

DICK *wears a wig.*

DICK: A tree walks into a bar and the barman says—you having the usual, Russell? And the tree says—if my wife rings tell her you just saw me leaf. Now no. That was funny. You have to admit that was good. That was funny. You should have a laugh sometimes. Release a bit of tension. Relax. Chill. Have a laugh. Force yourself. Fuck you. You're a difficult man to find. And don't say you weren't hiding. Because that's a matter of opinion. What do I want? Go on. Ask me. I want to ask you something. Do you get off on torturing people? I get no pleasure out of torturing people. Because that's normal. What do you call turning up at someone's lovely house and acting the fucking goat? Telling lies—saying dirty words? You've been making crank phone calls from a payphone. Hanging up before decent people get a chance to answer. How about opening people's private mail? Do you get off on that? And don't look at me. Because I'm a phantom. I'm a ghost. You can't see me. But you sure as fuck need me. A certain party organised for you to get treatment at a private health facility. All you had to do was admit what you'd been doing—promise to stop—and take the treatment. That's what she wanted. Do you remember her? You've been sitting here putting shiny silver trails all over her stolen aquamarine knickers. It's an illness. Don't beat yourself up about it. You're unwell. Her panties. I can't bring myself to say it. The bile rises too fast. What did you do with her coat? Did you torch your car and tell the pigs it was stolen? You're scared. Now it's all caught up with you. Look at you. You should get some fresh air. You don't look well. Which of your personalities am I talking to at the moment? Some people have a grasp on how short life is. They realise that being significant outweighs all other considerations. Some people don't. And one day they die insignificantly. Which are you? What is it you hoped to gain from this torment of your shit-pot remote torture amateur psychology? Because you know what you achieved? I will put you in a sleeper hold. I will put you in a stranglehold that will make your balls drop. You even mention her name and I will descend on you with the wrath of the righteous. If you'd made your apologies, your confessions, and concentrated on getting well—I don't think I live in the same world as you. I don't think I want to. On my planet I'm king and you are first up against the wall. I'd like to have you on my planet—first up against the wall. Let me tell you what is going to happen here. You don't like the boot on the other foot, do you? Typical bully coward creeping around scared to go toe to toe. Well, hard luck. Because the boot is staying on the other foot and the toe is going right up your puckered arse. And if it's a staring contest you want, then you are pissing into the wind facing off against me.

DEZ: Are you wearing a wig? Is that a wig? On your head. Why are you wearing a wig? Are you bald?

DICK: That's how it's going to be. Hard man. Wig spotter. You're playing a dangerous game. You have a death wish. I have a licence. I will put a move on you only me and two Green Berets know. You will go down asking your mum to forgive you for shitting your nappy. You provoke me to it. You've gone mad. Mad because I found you in your lair. And don't you look pathetic. Shrunken. Like a ten-year-old boy's penis after a long chlorinated swim. You're not some big scary monster. You're a piss-little man with swollen ideas.

DEZ: Where do they get the hair from?

DICK: You see, it could have been quick, but now it's going to be slow.

DEZ: You know what you are. You're a joke. You're the illusion of calm. That's all. You're the illusion of safety. So people are confident enough to go to the shops. But you're a joke.

DICK: That was a very cruel thing to say.

DEZ: You're a joke. A façade.

DICK: I'm still the closest thing we've got to peace. [*He takes off the wig and puts on a pair of rubber gloves.*] She's pregnant. Did you know? And she is—hormonal as all hell. It's a kind of illness. Pregnancy. Like having a parasitic infection. Have you seen her husband? Looks like he's wanked himself half to death. So how it happened—Angela's pregnancy—is anyone's guess. Do you have anything you want me to tell anyone? Last words. Any symbolic gestures you wish to make? Any items of significance for future generations? Are there any sentimental objects you'd like me to pass on? If so—go and get them. But get them now.

♦ ♦ ♦ ♦ ♦

SCENE NINE

TIM *and* ANGELA.

TIM *is wearing his captain's uniform.* ANGELA *is just becoming visibly pregnant.*

TIM: Have you got big plans for your day?
ANGELA: I have.
TIM: Me too.
ANGELA: Well, you look great.
TIM: And so do you.
ANGELA: I'm going over to James' house.
TIM: Oh.
ANGELA: He's asked me to completely redecorate.
TIM: When did this happen?
ANGELA: Last week. I told you.
TIM: Did you? I don't remember.
ANGELA: Anyway. I am.
TIM: Doesn't Marjorie mind you redecorating her house?
ANGELA: I told you. It's a surprise.
TIM: Doesn't he think she will notice?
ANGELA: She's in the Swiss Alps for six weeks. Mont Blanc. Remember?
TIM: No.
ANGELA: She's getting an oil change.

> *They laugh.*

It takes six weeks for the…
TIM: I imagine it would.
ANGELA: Still—
TIM: Nothing can upset me today. Nothing can upset me because I am back.
ANGELA: You are. You absolutely are.

TIM: And I enjoy the Domestic routes so—
ANGELA: You will be back on International before you know it.
TIM: I'm happy on Domestic. It has its own challenges.
ANGELA: And I get to see more of you.
TIM: I have to do an overnight stay tonight.
ANGELA: I know.
TIM: But that is not going to be the norm.
ANGELA: I'm used to it.
TIM: Watch my golf handicap go down now I'm on Domestic.

She gives him a few finishing touches.

ANGELA: I made the booking.
TIM: Good. Booking for what?
ANGELA: La Terrine. For Saturday. You haven't forgotten?
TIM: It's your birthday.
ANGELA: Yes.
TIM: Have I spoiled the surprise now?
ANGELA: I made the booking.
TIM: The winter degustation.
ANGELA: Yes. And you will enjoy it.
TIM: I will. I love all those tiny agonising little bites. God forbid we would just eat a plate of food. No. Give me agonising little suggestions of what could have been, every time.
ANGELA: It was your suggestion.
TIM: Was it?
ANGELA: You love La Terrine.
TIM: That's true. I do.

They fall silent.

We are doing very well, aren't we? We are a success, you would say.
ANGELA: That's true.
TIM: Look at us. We are a success.
ANGELA: Yes we are.
TIM: I am flying a plane today. A couple of hundred people trusting me with their lives. Two hundred or so people trusting a complete stranger with their lives so that they can be a thousand miles away from wherever they were to begin with. Because the sense of movement is enough to provoke—hope. The sense of the possibility of movement

is enough for us to put our lives in another's hands. I sometimes wish we hadn't invented flight.

ANGELA: No you don't.

TIM: Yes I do.

ANGELA: What would you do?

TIM: I'd be a baker.

ANGELA: And you would be miserable.

TIM: Yes. But it would be real.

ANGELA: Go to work.

TIM: I passed my psych assessment by one point.

ANGELA: What do you mean?

TIM: I mean they measure you empirically. My mind is measurable. And I fell one point within acceptability. I can be measured. So can you.

ANGELA: I don't think so. It was just a hoop for you to jump through.

TIM: And I jumped through. But I dragged my balls on the hoop somewhat. Still. I made it.

ANGELA: It's only normal that you are a little nervous.

TIM: You can be a bit cold, Angela. I don't mind, I suppose. But nevertheless, you are. Something about you—you're a little cold. Have you always been?

ANGELA: Not always. No.

TIM: You know, one day—someday—in the near future—we should have a long conversation. We should have a really long and open discussion about our hopes and fears.

ANGELA: I'd like that very much.

TIM: We should really try and connect.

ANGELA: Yes please. I want that.

TIM: We should tell each other everything. Our darkest filthiest secrets. Yes?

ANGELA: Yes please.

TIM: Do you believe we can?

ANGELA: Yes I do.

TIM: Yes. Me too. And I will draw diagrams.

They laugh.

ANGELA: You're back at work. I'm back designing.

TIM: And everything is happy and clean.
ANGELA: As much as we can humanly hope for.
TIM: Then why do I feel like I need to peel my skin and rinse it in brine?
ANGELA: Because you're a good person.
TIM: No. I'm not. But I try.
ANGELA: And you succeed. As close as you can.
TIM: No more than you.
ANGELA: We both do everything we can.
TIM: I'm looking forward to getting in the air.
ANGELA: I know you are.
TIM: It's something not everyone gets to experience.
ANGELA: I love you.
TIM: Where did that come from?
ANGELA: It just did.
TIM: You love me.
ANGELA: I do.
TIM: And I love you.
ANGELA: Thank you.
TIM: Whoever you are. Whoever I am.
ANGELA: We're whoever we need to be.

TIM *laughs.*

TIM: We love each other. We're having a family. A child. We are safe. We are good people. And I should go. I don't want to be late first day back. Don't answer the door to any strangers.

They laugh.

So helpless, Angela.
ANGELA: It's over.
TIM: It's over. It is over.
ANGELA: It is.
TIM: And you forgive me?
ANGELA: There's nothing to forgive.
TIM: If I could go back in time—or forward—
ANGELA: I said I love you.
TIM: And I promise not to crash the plane.

They touch.

When I thought about it—as a young man—I'm not sure what I expected.

ANGELA: I'll be here when you get back.

TIM: Us. I'm happy, Angela. I am.

ANGELA: I am too. We both are.

TIM: I am so very happy.

ANGELA: Yes. We both are.

TIM: Just asking. Just setting my dial.

ANGELA: Yes.

TIM: Yes.

ANGELA: Yes.

TIM: Right. Yes.

ANGELA: Yes.

TIM: We're good.

ANGELA: Better than that.

TIM: We're great.

ANGELA: Yes.

TIM: Yes.

ANGELA: Yes.

TIM: Aren't we?

ANGELA: I want to think so.

TIM: We're good people.

ANGELA: Yes we are.

TIM *hesitates.*

If you want—if you do want to know—then you can.

TIM: We occasionally have to look the other way.

ANGELA: But if you really want to know…

TIM: We look away. And you could scream.

ANGELA: I could.

TIM: But you won't.

ANGELA: Not where I'll be heard. No. Not out loud. Not out loud.

THE END

*9 7 8 0 8 6 8 1 9 8 0 2 6 *